CLOTH
FROM FIBER
TO FABRIC

CLOTH
FROM FIBER
TO FABRIC

WRITTEN AND
ILLUSTRATED BY
WALTER BUEHR

WILLIAM MORROW AND COMPANY
NEW YORK 1965

BY THE SAME AUTHOR

BREAD, the Staff of Life
HARVEST OF THE SEA
THE MARVEL OF GLASS
MEAT, from Ranch to Table
OIL, Today's Black Magic
RUBBER, Natural and Synthetic
TIMBER! Farming Our Forests
UNDERGROUND RICHES, the Story of Mining
VOLCANO!
WONDER WORKER, the Story of Electricity

CONTENTS

A LOOK AT CLOTH

Cloth is a marvel of our civilization, but we take it for granted and few of us know how it is made. If you have a pocket microscope or even a reading glass, focus it upon the sleeve of your coat, a stocking, a handkerchief, or a bed sheet. You will discover that these fabrics are not all one piece, like paper or plastic, but are made up of thousands of finely spun threads, which cross each other and interlace in hundreds of different patterns.

Some fabrics are made of coarse, loosely twisted, fuzzy yarns, while the threads in others are fine, smooth, and tightly twisted. The colorful designs are achieved in two different ways. Some are woven, using yarns of different colors, into intricate patterns. Others are printed on the woven cloth. Yarns in a tweed or flannel jacket are joined together very differently from the way those in a sweater are joined. The jacket fabric is woven and the sweater is knitted. The fabric in a summer dress or sport shirt is made of fine yarn and is loosely woven so that

the air can easily pass through it. The cloth in a winter coat is closely woven of heavy, hairy yarns, which insulate the body against cold.

The cloth you are examining may be made of yarns spun from wool, cotton, flax, silk, or one of the man-made fibers like rayon or nylon. Some yarns are spun from a combination of several fibers, such as silk and wool or cotton and nylon. The linsey-woolsey cloth our ancestors knew was woven from mixed linen and woolen yarns. When cloth is woven on a modern loom, so many different effects are possible that it is often hard to tell which fiber the cloth is made of. There are thousands of fibers, each different from the others, each suited to a particular purpose.

THE FIRST WEAVERS

Nobody knows when man began to make cloth. Some remains of cloth have been discovered that date from the beginning of the Stone Age. How long weaving existed before that time is impossible to say, because the evidence must have rotted away hundreds of centuries ago. However, many archeologists believe that weaving, or at least plaiting, began with the discovery of fire. Using animal skins, sinews, and intestines, as well as wild grasses, vines, flax, and the fibers of hemp, coconut, and palm, prehistoric people plaited mats, baskets, nets, rope, and crude blankets.

Probably one of the first fibers used in weaving was wool. Around 6000 B.C. some early ancestor of ours, living in a cave and dressed in animal skins, discovered that the soft fleece of the sheep was much warmer and thicker than the hairy skin of other beasts. He noticed that the wild sheep in his valley stayed together in flocks, so he cornered a small flock, fenced them in, and found that they could easily be tamed and herded. Now he had a supply of fleece for clothing. As the owner of a flock, he had to provide pasturage and shelter for it, and so this nomad hunter gradually became a herdsman.

After a while the sheep owner learned to twist the wool fibers into long strands of yarn, at first using only his fingers, then a spindle. Next he interlaced these strands to make a loose, rough piece of cloth, which could be turned into a far better garment than the raw sheepskin.

Eventually one of these weavers constructed a loom. He suspended a row of twisted yarns, which we now call warps, from a horizontal tree branch and weighted each end with a little

11

stone to keep the yarns from tangling. The weaver pulled crosswise yarns, called the weft, over one warp and under the next, from one side of the loom to the other. Later he learned to tie the end of the crosswise yarn, or weft, to a piece of stick, so he could hold it more easily, thus producing the first shuttle. With another stick, called a batten, he pushed the weft against the previously woven weft, making a tightly woven fabric. This was the earliest, most primitive loom.

The wild nomadic horsemen of the Asian steppes also began to breed flocks of sheep. Poor forage and harsh living conditions prevented them from raising cattle, but sheep could survive these conditions. The sheep supplied the nomads with meat, and their fleece was woven into clothing, woolen tents, and carpets. These Asiatics invaded the Near East and brought the first knowledge of woven garments to Asia Minor. Phoenician traders carried bolts of the wool cloth as well as spindles, crude looms, and probably small flocks of ewes and rams, in their cargoes to the countries along the Mediterranean.

By the beginning of recorded history fine spinning and weaving were well established in India and other Eastern nations. Wall murals from ancient Babylon, Assyria, Persia, and Egypt clearly show weavers at work, using tools that indicate they were already complete masters of the art. As early as 4000 B.C. Babylonian weavers were producing wool garments, and by 2500 B.C. the raising of sheep for wool and trade in fleeces was a flourishing business in Mesopotamia. At about the same time, in 2700 B.C., according to an old Chinese tradition, a Chinese princess discovered how to unwind a silkworm's cocoon and made the first thread for silk weaving.

The use of cotton, too, goes back thousands of years. Archeologists have dug up records from long-buried ruins of Indian cities in the Indus Valley that prove cotton was grown and woven as early as 3000 B.C. Cotton-wrapped mummies have been found in such widely separated places as the Inca tombs of Peru and the Nile Valley of Egypt. Wonderfully fine linen was also woven in Egypt as long ago as 2500 B.C. Linen wrappings, found on an Egyptian mummy in an ancient tomb, have had 540 warp threads to the inch while, until very recently, the finest modern weave contained only 350 threads.

Around 500 B.C. the cotton plant reached the Mediterranean, where it spread quickly. Soon the Romans were wearing beautifully woven gowns made out of cotton imported from Egypt and Arabia. The traders who brought cotton to Europe claimed that the fiber was really the wool of tiny animals called Scythian sheep, which grew on the stalks of a plant called bombassium. The waving stalks, each with a sheep as its flower, bent over far enough for the sheep to graze on the grass around the plant. When they had cropped all the grass

14

they could reach, they died. Then the natives could pluck their wool.

The Romans introduced sheep raising, spinning, and weaving into their far-flung provinces.

Sheep breeding was especially successful in Spain, where the climate seemed perfect for it. After many hundreds of years this breeding resulted in the Spanish Merino sheep, which produced the finest wool in the world. In order to keep their monopoly on this fine wool, the Spaniards jealously guarded the Merino sheep for a long time. The penalty for smuggling one out of the country was death. At last, however, a few Merinos were sneaked across the Portuguese border, and today their descendants are found among flocks all over the world.

The Romans exported sheep and textile workers to their province of Britain shortly after 55 B.C. Eventually wool and cloth became the principal exports of England. Flocks of sheep were sent to her colonies of Australia and New Zealand so they could grow wool for England's expanding weaving industry. This was the beginning of the great sheep-raising stations in the southern hemisphere.

In the Middle Ages the Germans excelled in

weaving fine cotton cloth and exported it to France and England. But not until the late thirteenth century did raw cotton become known in England, and then for some time it was used only in making candlewicks.

By the early eighteenth century some English weavers, using cotton imported from Smyrna and Cyprus, were turning out such large quantities of fustian, a cloth made of cotton and linen, that the woolen weavers began to protest. In 1700 Parliament was persuaded by the wool manufacturers to pass a law making it illegal to sell cotton cloth in England, with fines of from five to twenty pounds. The woolen weavers were so powerful that the law was not repealed until 1736, thirty-six years later. However, cotton cloth was so popular that in another fifteen years, there were 30,000 cottage handweavers producing it in England.

The Indians of the American continents seem to have developed weaving independently of the

Old World. In Peru the Spanish conquistador, Pizarro, found that the fabrics woven by the Incas were far better than any the Spanish weavers of that time could produce. Their handsomely decorated vests, ponchos, loin-cloths, draperies, and blankets were woven from wild cotton or from the hair of the llama, alpaca, and vicuña, which inhabited the rocky valleys of the Andes.

Our own Navahos of the Southwest were weaving beautiful blankets, belts, and headbands when Coronado and his helmeted Spanish horsemen appeared in Arizona and New Mexico in 1540. The Navahos are still weaving them today on the same primitive looms they used five hundred years ago.

Sheep came to the New World with Columbus, by way of the West Indies. Cortes introduced them to Mexico, and Coronado brought along flocks of sheep to feed his troops during his expeditions in our Southwest. Some of them remained with Spanish colonists, and presently sheep were grazing all over our western mountains and plains.

The English and Dutch colonists who came to Virginia, New Amsterdam, and New England also brought sheep with them, and began spinning and weaving homespun. The British government, spurred on by English weavers, tried to forbid cloth making among the colonists, so they would have to buy expensive English-made fabrics. Patriotic Americans, even those who could afford expensive English broadcloth, insisted on wearing American homespun. George Washington had a flock of 800 sheep with Merino blood at Mount Vernon, and his staff wove at least a yard of cloth on his handlooms every day.

When supplies from England were cut off by the Revolution, small American mills began to furnish cloth to the colonials during the war, and the industry continued to grow afterward.

Today every state in the Union has its flocks of sheep. There are thirty million of them in the United States, and they produce three hundred million pounds of wool every year, the sixth largest yield in the world.

WEAVING BY HAND

Until the middle of the eighteenth century spinning and weaving were done in the home. At that time the three main fibers used were wool, cotton, and flax. Farmers raised flocks of sheep on the fields, sheared them once or twice a year, and spun the fleece into yarn. They raised crops of flax from which they got the fibers to make linen, and they imported bales of cotton so they could weave calico. A weaver worked on a slow-moving handloom set in a corner of his kitchen or parlor, and he sold the cloth he made to traders or merchants. By the

21

sale of this homespun the peasants and tenant farmers earned enough to eke out a living.

Before the invention of the spinning wheel in the fourteenth century spinning was a slow and difficult craft, performed with the crudest of tools—the cards, the distaff, and the spindle. The spinster, usually a woman, prepared the fiber for spinning in different ways, depending upon the kind used. For instance, wool required five operations. First, the raw wool had to be scoured by washing it with soap and water. Second, the spinster dyed the wool by boiling it in a pot of dye water. Third, after the dyed fleece was dry, she fluffed it and picked out the burrs, sticks, and dirt, which was called teasing. Fourth, she worked oil into the wool to make it easier to spin. Fifth, with two wooden paddles, each of which had one side filled with wire nails bent toward the handle, she carded the wool. Placing a handful of oiled wool between the nail-studded cards, she then drew them across each other several times. This straightened the tangled fibers of wool and made them all lie in the same direction, much as you brush or comb your tangled hair in the morning.

The spinster gathered up this layer of smoothed wool into a soft roll, called a rolag, and wrapped it around the end of a long stick, called a distaff, or rock. Fixing the other end of the distaff in her belt or holding it under her left arm, she then drew a slender length of the fiber, called a roving, from the rolag and fastened the end of it in a notch at the upper end of a rounded, foot-long stick, tapered at each end. This was the spindle, which was usually driven through a clay or stone ring to steady it and give it enough weight to make it revolve longer when it was twirled.

Holding the rolag as high as possible, the spinster rolled the spindle against her leg with her right hand and tossed it, spinning, into the air, so that it dangled from the length of roving. The whirling spindle twisted the roving and transformed it into strong thread. When it

stopped, the spinster drew more from the rolag and set the spindle twirling again. After she had twisted a length of yarn tightly enough, she removed the end from the notch at the top of the spindle and wound the thread around the lower part of it. Then she fastened more untwisted roving to the top notch, and the spinning continued.

Spinning with distaff and spindle was awkward, and a good deal of skill was required to make an evenly twisted yarn. It was also a very slow process. These problems were greatly reduced, however, when the spinning wheel was invented, sometime in the fourteenth century. The first one consisted of a large wheel attached to a frame on which a horizontal spindle was set. The wheel was placed at right angles to the spindle, and a single belt ran around the circumference of the wheel and the middle of the spindle. When the spinster spun the wheel, she also turned the spindle. That left both of her hands free to draw the roving evenly from the rolag. Later still, a better spinning wheel appeared—the familiar one that stood in every early colonial home. This machine permitted the spinster to sit alongside it and turn the big wheel with a foot treadle while she fed the roving to the whirling spindle from a distaff fixed to the frame.

The sketch shows how a length of roving was put through the end of a hollowed-out spindle (A), out through a hole (B), around a wire hook (C), which was attached to one of a pair of wooden wings, called fliers (D), and tied to the reel (E). As the reel was turned by a belt around the big wheel, the yarn was twisted and pulled through the hole by the revolving flier and wound onto the reel. To distribute the yarn evenly on the reel the spinster put it around each hook in succession. When she had enough

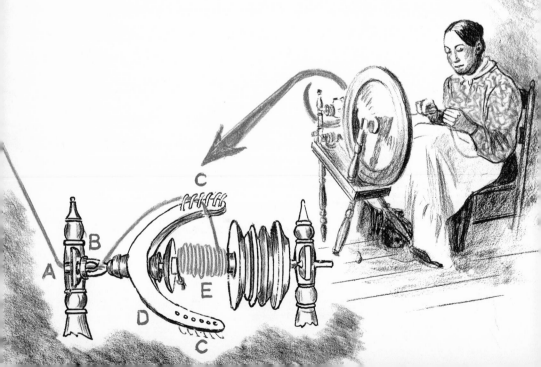

reels filled with spun yarn, she was ready to start weaving.

The illustration of an old English handloom shows how homespun cloth was woven. The loom has a strong wooden frame (X). Cross sticks (A) are placed so that alternate warps (lengthwise yarns) go over and under each stick, to prevent them from becoming tangled. (E) is the breast roller on which the fabric is wound as it is woven. This roller is fitted with a ratchet, which permits it to be turned only one way. (G) is the weaver's seat and (F) the treadles, used to raise and lower the heddles (B). (HJ) is a bar hung from two ropes, from which weights (K) are suspended. The other ends of these ropes are wound three times around (D) the cane roller, or loom beam, and also have weights tied to them. The weights keep pulling back on the loom beam, maintaining tension on the warps, whose ends are wound around the beam all along its length.

When the weaver sets up a loom, he spreads

the warp ends along a smooth stick, called the
cane stick, which fits into a groove in the loom
beam and is locked into place with another
stick. To spread the warps evenly, the weaver

28

threads the strands between the teeth of the raddle, which looks like a fine-toothed comb standing with its teeth upright. After the warp ends are distributed along the raddle, a cap is put over the teeth, locking them in place.

The weaver now threads the warps through the heddles, the most important part of the loom. The heddles are close-set, vertical bars of wood or wire, mounted in a frame, something like a picture frame. Every other heddle has a hole through it. When the loom is set up, the first warp passes through the hole in the first heddle; the next warp goes between that heddle and the adjacent one.

In a loom with a double heddle, used for plain weaving, the even-numbered warps pass through the holes in the first frame and the odd-numbered ones go between the heddles. In the second heddle frame the process is reversed: the odd-numbered warps pass through the holes, and the even-numbered ones go between.

Next the warps pass between the teeth of

the batten (C), a stick that also looks like a comb, with one warp to each space. Then the warp ends are fastened to the breast roller in the same way that the other ends are fixed to the loom beam.

Now the weaver steps on the treadle that pulls up the first heddle frame and all the even-numbered warps running through its holes. The even-numbered warps are now above the odd-numbered warps, which stay level because they run between the heddles. The warps now form a V-shaped space, called the shed, the even warps making the roof and the odd warps making the floor. The weaver takes in his left hand a small boat-shaped, hollowed-out piece of wood, called the shuttle. In the hollow of the shuttle is a revolving spool wound with yarn, which is called the weft. One end of the weft is fastened to the outside strand of warp at the left side of the loom. From left to right the weaver runs the shuttle through the shed formed by the odd- and even-numbered warps. As he

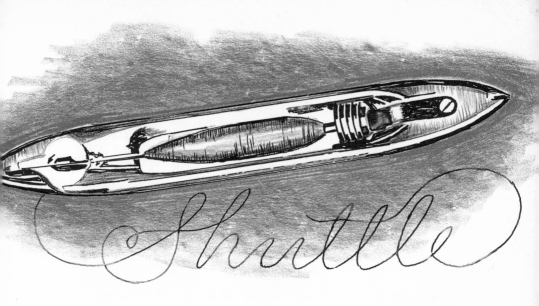

Shuttle

does so, the shuttle trails behind it one strand of the weft yarn.

Then the weaver presses down the other heddle, which pulls up all the odd-numbered warps in the second heddle frame, while the first frame returns to its original position. The weaver pushes the shuttle back through the tent again, but because the even-numbered warps are now lowered and the odd-numbered ones are raised, the weft passes behind each warp it previously passed in front of. This interlacing of warp and weft is weaving.

Each time the shuttle passes from one side to

31

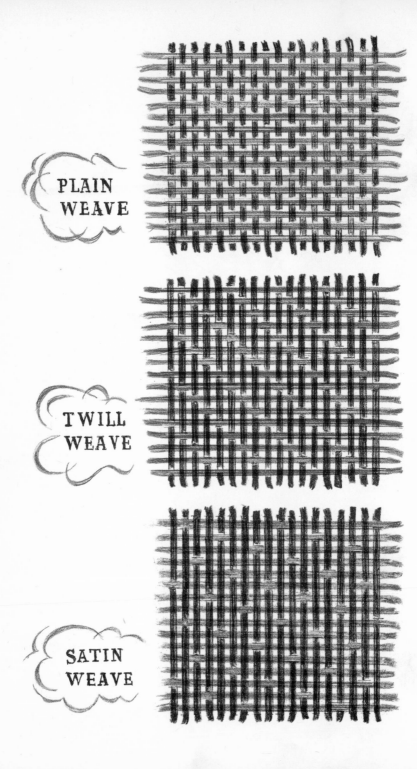

PLAIN
WEAVE

TWILL
WEAVE

SATIN
WEAVE

the other, the weaver pulls the batten toward him. The batten swings in an arc and pushes the newly woven weft against the preceding one, thus making a tight, smooth piece of cloth. By occasionally changing to a shuttle holding a different colored yarn, the weaver can form stripes or other patterns in the fabric. By varying the way in which the weft passes over and under the warp, he can achieve a different type of weave.

There are three basic weaves: plain, twill, and satin. In the plain weave, threads running in one direction go under and over alternate single threads running in the other direction. To make a twill weave, the weaver threads the heddle so that the weft goes under one warp and then over several at a time. In the satin weave, which is really only a variation of twill, the weft yarn passes many warps at a time. The finished fabric looks shiny, because the many threads all running in the same direction catch the light.

WEAVING BY MACHINE

No matter how skilled the weaver, weaving was still slow and costly. As a result, men with inventive minds began tinkering with machines that would improve and speed up the ancient craft. One of the first inventions was the fly shuttle, patented on May 26, 1733, by John Kay, an English machinist. Formerly a weaver had to pass the shuttle from one hand to the other through the shed, and if broadcloth was being woven—so called because it was wider than the usual thirty-inch width, the limit of one man's reach—two men were needed, one to stand at each side, so they could cast the shuttle back and forth to each other. But a single weaver could cast John Kay's fly shuttle from side to side of the loom. Using two cords and a lever, the weaver worked the shuttle with one hand and the batten with the other.

However, John Kay's invention brought him nothing but trouble. The large cloth makers copied the fly shuttle without paying him anything. While he won every suit he brought against them, he was almost bankrupted by the cost of the suits. At the same time the small cottage weavers were afraid that his shuttle would put them out of work. A mob of them broke into the house where John Kay had set up his machines. They destroyed everything they could find and would also have killed him if he had not been smuggled out under a sheet by friends. He fled to France, where he died in poverty, although the machines he invented are still being used today.

Presently the looms, improved by Kay's invention, were producing cloth so fast that the hand spinners could no longer keep up with the demand for yarn. Several inventors produced machines to spin yarn, but the first practical spinning machine was invented by a poor weaver and carpenter named James Hargreaves.

The idea for his machine came to Hargreaves one day when he saw his small daughter Jenny overturn a one-thread spinning wheel. When the spinning wheel fell, the horizontal spindle was placed in an upright position, where it continued to revolve. Hargreaves suddenly realized that if a number of spindles were placed upright, side by side, more threads could be spun at the same time. After many trials he finally produced such a machine, which he called a spinning jenny in honor of his daughter. This machine could spin eight threads at once. Later improved models turned out as many as 120 threads at once. However, the spinning jenny was unable to spin thread strong enough to be used as warp and so could be used only for weft.

The next spinning machine came from another Englishman, Richard Arkwright. He was born in 1732 and went to work while he was still a boy. He was first apprenticed to a barber and later opened a basement barbershop in a northern English city called Bolton.

Arkwright was always more interested in mechanics than in barbering, and in 1769 he patented a new spinning frame. In this machine the roving passed between sets of rollers, one of which turned faster than the other and made it possible for the roving to be twisted by the

Arkwright's original water frame—1769

spindles into thread strong enough to use as warp. His invention produced such good yarn that he opened the first cotton mill in the world in Nottingham. This spinning frame was a power machine in contrast to the earlier hand machines. That is, it ran continuously on a belt drive operated by horses in treadmills. Hand machines were worked by the hands and feet of a human being. Arkwright was so successful that he was knighted, and he became the first millionaire in the fabric industry.

Another important man in the growing textile industry was Samuel Crompton. An Englishman, he was born near Bolton on December 3, 1753. He came from a family of spinners and weavers, and his widowed mother was so poor that she had to put him to work at a loom as soon as his feet could reach the treadles. Like other weavers, he worked with yarn produced by Arkwright's spinning frame. It was often coarse and soft, and it broke easily on the loom. Samuel's mother scolded him for losing so much time joining the constantly breaking yarn, and so he began to think of some way to improve and strengthen it. For five years, from his twenty-first to his twenty-sixth year, he worked on his machine in a cold gloomy attic, often late at night after everybody else had gone to bed.

At last Crompton completed his machine, which he called a mule, because it was the result of a cross between the spinning jenny and the spinning frame, as a mule is a cross between a mare and a donkey. Crompton's mule stretched the thread as it came from the rollers before winding it on the spindle, which made it much stronger.

The yarn Crompton made was a success, and he got high prices for it. Everybody wanted to know the secret of his spinning machine, and some people climbed ladders to his attic, so they could spy through the windows at it. One man even climbed to the roof and bored a hole in it, so he could peep down at the machine. To hide the mule from these spies, Crompton had to put screens around it.

Crompton never had enough money to secure a patent, so presently the mule was copied by spinners everywhere, with very little payment to him. Cloth making made others rich, and weavers grew so prosperous that they walked the streets smoking long churchwarden pipes, with five-pound notes stuck in their hatbands. When they sat down in the public room of an inn, they insisted that the innkeeper clear out everybody except weavers.

At one time the looms equipped with Kay's fly shuttle could consume more yarn than could be spun. Now the mule was able to spin more yarn than the slow handlooms could use. Something had to be done to speed up weaving. Edmund Cartwright, a Church of England minister, solved the problem.

Cartwright, born at Nottingham on April 24, 1743, was not an inventor, knew nothing of mechanics, and had never even seen a loom.

However, one day in 1784, quite by accident, he heard some gentlemen from Manchester talking about the need for thousands of hand-looms, if the weaving trade was to keep up with the growing demand for cloth, and the impossibility of finding enough trained weavers to run them. Cartwright told them that Arkwright, who had invented the spinning frame, should now get busy and invent a power loom.

Later he remembered the conversation and began to think. As far as he knew, a loom had only three movements, which followed each other in constant succession. Deciding he could design a power machine that would perform those three simple movements, Cartwright began to sketch ideas for a loom, and presently hired a blacksmith and a carpenter to bring his drawings to reality. When the loom was finished, he hired a weaver to put in the warp, and was ready to begin his experiment. He set the machine in motion and, to his joy, produced a perfectly satisfactory piece of sailcloth.

Unfortunately, Cartwright had to make the springs and other parts of his loom so stiff and heavy that it took two strong men to operate it. He took out a patent, anyway, on April 4, 1785, and then for the first time inspected other looms and realized the many mistakes he had made. He continued to work on his loom, mak-

MODEL OF CARTWRIGHT'S POWER LOOM

A warp beam
B cloth beam
C boxes with springs to throw shuttles
D cylinder which operates loom

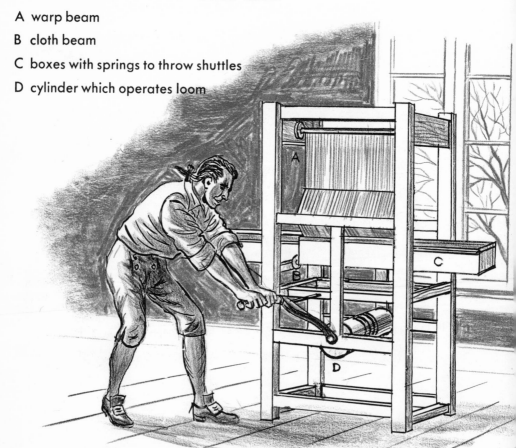

Hand crank replaced by belt on actual machines.

ing changes in it and perfecting it, and in 1787 took out another patent. His final loom not only produced fabrics with power machinery, it stopped automatically when a thread broke. The most skilled machinists in the weaving trade had not been able to create such a machine, and its principles are still in use today.

Manufacturers showed little interest in buying Cartwright's looms, so he finally set up his own shop at Doncaster. At first he powered his looms by a bull on a treadmill. Later he replaced the bull with an early steam engine, its boiler fired by alcohol. Without ever having seen any other engines, he proceeded to make a number of original and useful improvements on his.

In 1790 Cartwright built a new mill with 400 of his looms, operated by steam. Then ill fortune struck. The handweavers of that time looked upon any improvements in machines with terror. They saw how much more power machines could produce than their own slow handlooms, and they believed that they would soon be put out of work by them. They did not realize that the machines would actually create more jobs, because they could produce cloth so cheaply that more people all over the world could afford to buy it. The handweavers saw only the immediate threat, and so mobs gathered throughout Lancashire, smashing and burning the mills and power machines. In 1790 Cartwright's mill was attacked and burned to the ground. The loss of his capital and the ill will of the weavers finally caused him to give up the textile business in discouragement. He turned to inventing farm implements, and after being given a tardy reward of ten thousand pounds by Parliament for his remarkable invention of the power loom, he bought a farm to which he retired.

By the beginning of the nineteenth century all the machines necessary to weave cloth—the carding and combing machines, the spinning frames, and the looms—had been invented. They were so well designed that only minor improvements have been made in them right up to the present day. However, there was not always enough power to run them. In England the water power was limited, and steam engines were as yet not powerful enough to run machinery efficiently.

James Watt, who was born in 1736, finally solved this problem. Originally apprenticed to a maker of scientific instruments, Watt later made mathematical instruments for Glasgow College. Here he was once called on to repair a model of the crude steam pump invented by Thomas Newcomen, which was used to pump water from the mines of Cornwall.

Watt realized at once that Newcomen's engine was so badly designed that it wasted enormous quantities of coal and steam, and he saw how it might be improved. He set to work on a model, and in 1769 took out a patent on the engine that led eventually to the steamship and the locomotive. His first model was designed to drive only steam pumps for the mines, but with later improvements it was able to drive machinery of all kinds, including spinning machines and power looms. This was the last step necessary for the successful operation of fabric mills.

FACTORY WEAVING

By the nineteenth century the industrial revolution was in full swing. Home spinning and weaving had almost died out.

Most weaving was now done in factories. Some manufacturers, looking for greater profits, cut the wages of their mill hands, who then had to work longer hours for a living wage. Other manufacturers, in order to compete with the lower prices of the sweatshop operators, had to cut their wages too. Presently the workers' wives, sons, and daughters were also bent over the spindles and looms. Even young children of eight and nine worked for twelve and four-

teen hours a day in the noisy, dust-laden mills, because their parents desperately needed the few pennies they could earn.

In eighteenth- and nineteenth-century America the same working conditions developed in the mills of New England. Backwoods farm families left their stony, worn-out farms and came to the towns to work in the mills, where they worked equally hard. Gradually laws were passed forbidding the hiring of young children and limiting the working hours of women and girls. Labor unions were organized, and they fought bitterly with the owners of the factories for better wages and a shorter working day. These very victories of the workers, however, were soon to lose them their jobs.

At first the weaving and knitting mills were all located in the Northeast, mostly in New England, where there were more people with the money to build factories. There were also more towns in this section, and the mills could find the necessary skilled workers in them. New England also had a large number of fast-running rivers with which to drive mill wheels.

But by the twentieth century high wages and strong unions made it expensive to weave cloth in the Northeast. Northern mill owners began closing their plants in New England and moving to the South, which had specialized in raising cotton. There they could build and run factories more cheaply because of the milder climate. By locating their plants close to the cotton plantations they could cut the cost of shipping cotton to the mill. They also found it cheaper to hire Southerners put out of work by mechanized farming than to pay the wages demanded by the unions in the North. Today most of the spinning and weaving mills have left New England and are now located in the South.

KNITTING

There are a number of ways to make fabric, but the two basic methods of combining yarns are weaving and knitting. Although knitting was done in ancient times in some parts of the world, it was unknown in Europe before the fifteenth century. Stockings used to be made of woven fabric. The sewer cut a double thickness of the fabric to a pattern of the leg. Then he sewed the fabric together making a long seam at the back. The Scots claim to have invented knitting and to have introduced it into France and England. Even today one can see old Scots-men knitting sturdy woolen stockings.

Knitting is done by interlocking loops of

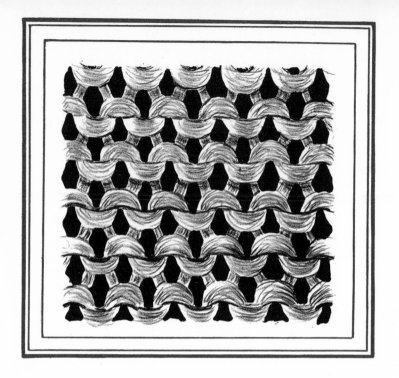

yarn with large needles, instead of crossing warp and weft at right angles as in weaving. The needles have been made of bone, wood, steel, ivory, and celluloid. Two needles with heads are used for flat, or selvage, work. Three or more needles, pointed at both ends, are used for circular knitting, as in making stockings. For large tubular-shaped work a circular needle is used.

The first machine to knit stockings was designed by the Reverend William Lee of St.

John's College in Cambridge, England, in the 1580's. He invented it for a very curious reason. While courting a young lady of the town, he felt that she was paying too much attention to her knitting and not enough to his wooing. Jealously he resolved, then and there, to invent a machine that would put his rival, hand knitting, out of business.

It is strange how often ministers have invented successful machines for making cloth. Reverend Lee's machine was one of these successes. By 1589 he had completed it, but, to his misfortune, it could knit only heavy, coarse wool stockings. When he applied to Queen Elizabeth for a patent, she refused to grant it to him, because the stockings his machine made were no better than the kind many of the Queen's poor subjects knit by hand to earn their bread. She refused to give him a monopoly at their expense, but said that if his machine could have knitted fine silk stockings, which only a few of her more prosperous sub-

jects could afford, she would have been inclined
to give him his patent.

Lee went back to his bench and by 1598 completed another machine that *could* make fine

silk stockings. He presented a pair to the Queen, who admired them, but for some reason she gave Lee neither patent nor reward. Discouraged, he finally went to France to open a factory, at the invitation of King Henry IV. But bad luck still dogged him. In 1610, before Lee could establish himself, the king was assassinated, and he received no more help from the Crown. He died, a pauper, in Paris the same year.

Lee's brother took his machine back to England, where in 1657 Oliver Cromwell granted it a charter. Later it was much improved by Jedediah Strutt, who opened a knitting mill at Derby. Strutt's knitting mill became the largest in England.

In modern machine knitting all knitted fabrics can be divided into two classes—circular knit and flat knit. A circular, or tubular knit, is so called because the fabric is knitted around a circular machine in tubular form. These tubular-shaped fabrics range from narrow braid to pieces of material forty inches wide. When a circular fabric is hand knit, it is made from one single, continous yarn, or thread. When it is machine knit, a number of threads, each of which in turn makes an entire row of loops around the edge of the fabric, are used. After the knitting is finished, the fabric is cut from top to bottom and becomes a flat piece of material.

Flat knitting is done in several different patterns. The most common is called warp knitting. In it the needles pick up individual threads, which are strung out parallel and flat, and loop them to other threads with a zigzag motion. In weft, or filling, knitting, as in hand knitting, the fabric is constructed in horizontal rows with one continous yarn. The basic stitches are plain, or jersey, purl, and rib.

The gauge number in a stocking indicates the number and size of knitted rows to an inch. As the gauge increases, there are more rows to an inch, the thread is finer, the number of loops in a row increase, and the loops become smaller. The denier number indicates the fineness of yarn used; thirty denier is a coarser yarn than twenty.

Two different needles are used in knitting machines—the spring needle and the latch needle, which are illustrated here to show their action.

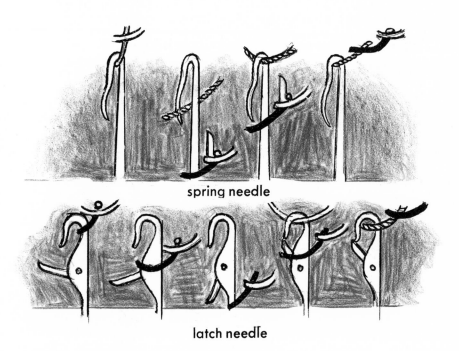

spring needle

latch needle

BLEACHING AND DYEING

After cloth has been woven on a loom, it is usually discolored and stained by plant juices mixed with the fiber. Until it has been bleached white it is unfit for dyeing or printing. In England the people who did the bleaching were called whitsters.

The early bleaching of linen was a curious craft. First a whitster soaked the cloth in sour milk and cow's dung. Then he poured boiling potash lye over it and steeped it in the lye water for a week's time. This was called buck-

58

ing. In India a mixture of lemon juice and buffalo milk was used to buck cloth.

After bucking, the whitster thoroughly washed the linen and soaked it in vats of buttermilk for five or six days. Last of all he spread the long strips of linen out on the grass and exposed them to the sun and rain for several months, an operation that was called crofting. Altogether the bleaching process might take as long as eight months, during the spring, summer, and autumn. Although it was slow, no other method has ever bleached linen as dazzlingly white. The sight of thousands of yards of fine, expensive cloth lying on the grass out of doors was too great a temptation for some to resist. So much linen was stolen that a law, passed in the reign of George II, made the theft of any fabric being bleached punishable by death.

Eventually it was discovered that cloth could be bleached with various chemicals, such as sulfuric acid, lime, and chlorine. So, with faster methods, the picturesque old ways of bleaching have almost disappeared, although they are still used in Ireland, which is famous for its fine linens.

Dyeing is an ancient craft. The Chinese, Persians, and Indians used dyes many centuries ago, and perhaps the Phoenicians and Egyptians used them even earlier. In the thirteenth and fourteenth centuries dyeing became important in Italy, where the craft was perfected. From Italy skilled dye masters spread through the rest of Europe, taking their knowledge with them.

Dye masters dipped or boiled yarns from

bleaching linen

which colored fabrics would be made in dye kettles. Until the nineteenth century they used only natural dyes. They were obtained from insects, animal blood, colored earth or minerals, and the juices of roots, berries, and leaves. Red came from the roots of the madder plant. One kind of blue, probably the oldest dye known, came from the indigo plant. Another blue was made by boiling the leaves of a plant called woad. Walnut juice supplied brown. The uniforms of the Confederate soldiers in the American Civil War were dyed brown with butter-

nut juice. Tyrian purple, the imperial color, came from a species of snail. Cochineal, a brilliant scarlet, was made from the bodies of certain insects native to Mexico. Prussian blue, ocher, and umber were made from colored earths.

Modern dyeing is done almost entirely with aniline or synthetic dyes obtained from coal tar. Fabrics like silk and wool take to dyes so well that they can be dipped into the dye kettle without any special preparation. When material like cotton must be dyed, a mordant is also used. It fixes the color so that it won't wash out.

Instead of painstakingly weaving a design into a fabric by using different colored yarns, it was also possible to print it on the material after it was woven, just as pictures are printed on paper. Textile printing originated in China and India, and was also known to the Indians of Peru, Chile, and Mexico. First the craftsman cut a design in a wood block. Then he ran an ink-filled roller over the block and pressed it on the fabric, using a different block for each color.

Hand block printing was done in Europe in the early seventeenth century, and in 1734 a Frenchman named Perrot, of Rouen, built a machine that could print textiles from blocks. By 1770 fabrics were being printed from metal plates on which the designs were engraved. Fifteen years later an Englishman named Bell engaved his designs on curved plates, which he mounted on a cylinder. By revolving the cylinder and running a moving strip of cloth underneath it, he was able to print a pattern continuously on the cloth. With some slight improvements, this method is still being used today.

WOOL

Wool fiber has many characteristics that make it ideal for weaving into cloth. Each fiber is covered with a layer of overlapping scales. They surround an inner packing, called the cortex, which is made up of millions of small spindles, or cortical cells. Some of the coarser wool fibers have a hollow space in the center, called the medulla.

Because of the scales on the outside of each wool fiber, a garment made of it resists a certain amount of rain or snow. At the same time the inner cells of the wool fiber absorb the moisture of the body in the form of vapor and let it escape through the scales to the outer atmosphere. That is why a wool shirt remains relatively dry when the wearer perspires heavily, while a shirt made of cotton or silk becomes wringing wet and sticks to the skin.

Another advantage of wool is its resilience. Wool fibers lie in a natural corkscrew shape. Even a gentle pull will straighten them out, but they will spring back again as soon as one end is released. In addition, wool fibers are com-

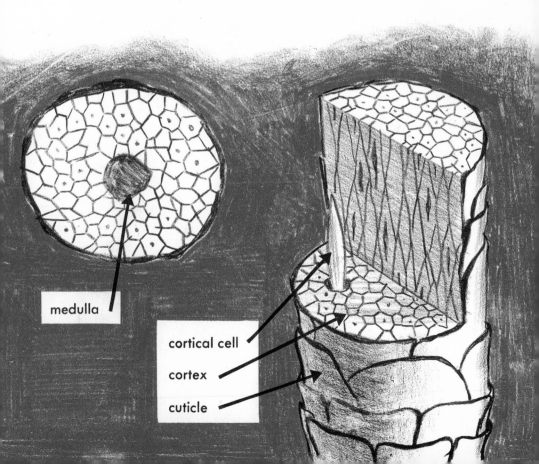

medulla

cortical cell

cortex

cuticle

posed of millions of chain molecules, much too tiny to see, which also lie naturally in crimps. These molecules straighten out when the cloth is pulled, but return to their corkscrew shape when the pull stops. That is why badly wrinkled wool clothes smooth out when they are hung for some time from a hanger.

Wool fibers tend to spring away from each other when they have been woven into cloth. This action keeps the fabric from matting, and the thousands of spaces between the yarn fibers are filled with dead air, which is a fine insulation. As everyone knows, a wool garment keeps out cold air in the winter, but it can also insulate the body from heat in the summer. Desert Arabs, for example, cover themselves completely with hoods and robes of wool.

Wool also resists static electricity, which makes garments cling, and it is durable.

Wool garments, by Act of Congress, must be labeled to indicate the condition of the wool used. The labels *Virgin Wool* and *New Wool* mean that the fiber has never been converted into yarn or fabric before. *Wool* means that the fiber has never been woven before, although it may be reclaimed from wool that was partly processed. *Reprocessed Wool* is fiber reclaimed from scraps of wool fabrics that have never been worn. *Reused Wool* is fiber made from old clothes and rags, usually blended with some new wool to give the fabric strength.

Wool fabrics can be woven from any of the above grades of wool, or from wool fibers combined with other types of fibers, such as silk, linen, cotton, nylon, Dacron, or Dynel. These mixtures of yarns have certain advantages, such as resistance to shrinking, over all-wool yarn.

Not all wool is the same. There are many varieties, each with different qualities, and the weaver must carefully choose the one that fits his special needs. In the first place, different breeds of sheep produce different kinds of wool, and there are two hundred breeds of sheep in the world, thirteen of them in the United States.

Some sheep are raised only for their wool. Others are also used as a source of meat, and generally they yield a lower grade of wool than those bred only for their fleece. Sheep raised in cool, damp climates usually produce a better grade of wool than those raised in hot, dry climates. Also, the better the flocks are fed and cared for, the better the wool. The length of the wool fibers is very important, too. Only long-fibered wool, from certain breeds, can be used to make wor-

1 sides

2 withers

3 loin (best)

4 hind quarters ⎫
⎪
5 belly ⎬ (short, stiff, and straight)
⎪
6 throat ⎭

7 shins ⎫
⎬ (short and dirty)
8 head ⎭

sted fabric. Worsted cloth is smoother and of a finer quality and lighter weight than other wool fabric.

Even the location of the wool on the sheep's body affects its quality. For instance, wool from the loins is better than wool from the hind-quarters. The sketch of a sheep shows the various areas and their quality.

The colors of fleeces vary, from pure white to a dirty, yellowish brown. Only white wool can be used to make white fabrics, and batches to be dyed must be carefully matched to prevent variations after dyeing.

Once and sometimes twice a year the big sheep ranches round up their flocks and run the

sheep, one by one, through a shack where an expert shearer awaits them with his electric clippers. With a few quick motions he separates the animal from its fleece, and the baaing, naked sheep is sent back out on the range to grow a new coat.

The fleece, all in one piece, tangled and dirty, full of burrs and leaves, is then laid on a table before the sorter, a man who is expert at separating it into the various grades of wool. He

tears apart the fleece and tosses handfuls of wool into different baskets, according to the length of the fibers, the fineness, the strength, and the color. When the baskets are full, the contents are dumped into huge sacks, labeled as to grade, and shipped to the company's warehouse in some city.

Here the sorted wool gets a bath in a big tank of hot soapy water to wash out the dirt, salts, and grease. The grease, which the sheep itself produces to coat its wool, is called lanolin, and is sold to the makers of face creams, soaps, and other products. The scoured wool is then baled and shipped to a mill warehouse.

THE MODERN
WOOLEN MILL

Although the carders, spinning frames, and looms in a modern mill look—and are—very complicated, they work on exactly the same principles as the distaffs, spindles, and crude looms of centuries ago. Today's machines, however, work very much faster. The first power machines of the late eighteenth century were so well designed that they have only needed minor improvements since that time. Recently a Swiss invented new machinery which weaves cloth even faster and in a different way, but it is the first significant change in weaving since the power loom was invented.

A Maryland mill that weaves fine worsteds and woolens for suits, sport coats, topcoats, and overcoats is perhaps typical of the modern woolen mill. This mill, which has been producing fine cloth for many years, stands in a valley. Far up the valley behind a dam is a pond. A millrace over a mile long delivers water from the pond to the mill wheel at the plant. Many mills, like this one, still use water power, but a modern turbine wheel, housed in the mill basement, replaces the moss-grown, creaking, wooden waterwheel.

As we approach this mill we can hear the roar of the water leaving the millrace. At one time the power of the mill wheel was transferred to the machines by long shafts and slapping leather belts. Now the turbine drives a big dynamo, making electricity to run electric motors.

A visit to the mill begins in a room where inspectors comb out tufts of dyed wool and compare their color to that of small numbered samples, which have been sent to the mill by customers. The dye master must match them exactly.

This mill buys its wool from a company that

sends its buyers all over the world to bid on the wool crop in Australia, Scotland, or perhaps Argentina. Burlap-covered bales are stacked high along the walls of its warehouse. Some of the bales look different from the others. Their contents are brilliantly white, and their texture is even and compact, unlike the lumpy wool. These bales hold man-made fibers, like nylon or Orlon, which will be blended with the wool fibers to make special yarns.

From the warehouse the wool goes to the dyeing room. Sometimes wool is not dyed until after it has been spun into yarn, or until it has been woven into piece goods—bolts of cloth, sold later by the yard to retail customers. In this mill the stock is top-dyed, which means it is dyed before spinning.

The tangled blobs of wool are dumped out and sorted for color, because white wool takes color differently from yellowish wool. If they are spun together, the result is a mottled yarn. The sorted wool fibers are loaded into wheeled

trucks and trundled to the great shining dye
kettles. In five-hundred-pound lots the wool is
dumped into the kettles. The dye powders for
each batch have been carefully weighed and
mixed in the mixing room according to a formula worked out by the dye master. The formula
will match a sample previously made and ap-
proved by the customer. The dye is mixed with

hot water and piped into the dye kettle containing the wool. The kettle is watched over by an electric timing device, which turns the heat on and off at exactly the right instant. Nylon and other man-made fibers don't take dye as readily as wool does. They must be dyed separately in a special kettle under high pressure.

Next the dyed wool is run through long troughs filled with water where the excess dye is washed out. Then it is put through a drier. This process is also exactly timed. Too short a drying period turns out wool too damp to work, while too much drying makes it brittle. Yarn spun from brittle wool breaks easily in the loom.

After drying, the wool goes to the mixing room. Here are trucks heaped with twists of wool, colored in various tones of blue, brown, gray, black, yellow, and red. When two or more colored wools are to be twisted into one strand of yarn, they must be thoroughly blended into a uniform combination. The blobs of wool are passed between cylinders, faced with tiny wire teeth, which separate them into little tufts. The tufts are then piped into a high-ceilinged room where a giant fan creates a wool "blizzard" and mixes them thoroughly. If the mixture doesn't exactly match the sample, more wool of another color may be added until it does.

At this stage the wool is a tangled mass of fibers, which must now be carded and combed. The wool is run between revolving cylinders with fine wire teeth, which do the job of the cards once used by hand spinners. The wire teeth remove any burrs or twigs and straighten out the tangled fibers. To make worsted yarn, the long-fibered wool is combed to remove any short fibers and to make the long fibers lie parallel. This treatment makes it easier to twist the wool into a thin, tight, smooth-surfaced yarn later.

After the wool is carded and combed, it emerges in a long, fluffy, even band called a web. The web is split into long thin strands, called roving, that have not yet been twisted and have no strength. The roving now goes to the spinning frame, or jenny, where it passes between rollers. This operation reduces its size. Then the roving is twisted by the spindles and wound on large bobbins. The wool, which is now strong yarn, is rewound on smaller bobbins before it is ready for the weaving loom. By making the yarns lighter or heavier, or by twisting them tightly or loosely, different kinds of fabrics are created.

Next the bobbins of yarn are set up in a dressing frame. Beyond the dressing frame is a kind of giant spool, called the warping beam. The end of each strand of yarn is threaded through one of a row of wire eyes, which keep all the warps parallel to each other. Then the yarn is wound around the warping beam.

The dresser arranges the order of the yarns for winding according to a pattern he has been given. It may call for three strands of gray yarn, then one white strand, followed by four of blue. This order is repeated over and over across the

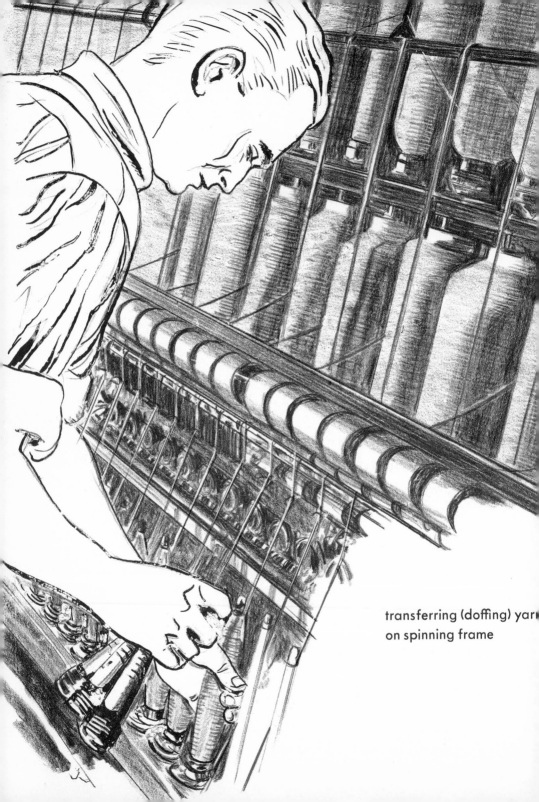

transferring (doffing) yar[n]
on spinning frame

full width of the frame, so that now one sees a colored pattern of stripes made up of yarns running only in one direction. The dressing frame begins to look something like a giant particolored spider web.

When the yarn has all been wound on the warping beam, little groups of the ends are tied together to keep them from tangling. Then an empty loom beam, another huge spool, is snapped into place alongside the warping beam. The ends of the yarn are untied and fastened to the loom beam in exactly the same relation to each other as before. As the beams revolve, the warping beam transfers the yarn to the loom beam. Again the ends are tied together, and again the loom beam is set in place in the power loom.

The weaver once more unties the dangling ends of the warps and pulls each one through an eye or a slot in the heddles, which are mounted in harness frames, just as in the old English handloom. There are some differences;

modern power looms sometimes use as many as twenty-two harness frames to make fabrics with elaborate patterns, and the frames are automatically raised and lowered.

Because the looms move so fast, much yardage would be spoiled if the machine kept on weaving after a yarn broke. Therefore, each warp passes through a hole in a little metal strip, called a drop wire. As soon as a warp breaks, the drop wire falls, which instantly stops the loom.

A shuttle carries the weft, just as it did on the old handloom, at right angles across the warp, through the tent made when the heddles in the harness frames lift up some of the warp. This process is called picking. The big difference today, of course, is in the operation of the shuttle. Instead of being passed back and forth from hand to hand, as it used to be, the modern shuttle flies back and forth on a little ledge alongside the reed, or batten. At each side a picker stick bats it back, like a bat striking a baseball, and it flies so fast that the eye sees only a flash.

At one side of the shuttle path is a magazine holding a number of shuttles, each with a different color yarn on its spool. By means of a chain drive the magazine is raised or lowered so that the shuttle with the proper yarn is in position to be batted across at just the right time. The spools of yarn in the shuttles are also renewed automatically without stopping the loom.

The three main weaves are shown in the diagram. First, the plain weave is used in making taffeta, chambray, seersucker, sheeting, poplin, organdy, and flat crepe. Second, the twill weave is used for serge, covert, foulard, tweed, flannel, and gabardine. Third, the satin weave, a variation of the twill, is used for satin material. It gets its sheen by floating one yarn end across four or more of the warp threads.

Endlessly different patterns can be made by using more harness frames and more shuttles, threaded with yarns of a different weight, finish, or color, or twisted at different tension. Fabrics with patterns of small figures sometimes need as many as twenty-two harness frames. Large elaborate patterns are woven on the Jacquard loom, on which the weaving of the designs is controlled by punched cards. Electric needles, passing through the punched holes in the cards, complete circuits that cause the proper heddles to be lifted at the right instant and permit a weft yarn to be woven over the warp at the right place.

After the cloth has been woven into long strips, it passes through the fulling machine. Here, in a vat containing alkali or acid, it runs between rollers, which first bunch up the cloth, then stretch it out, repeating the operation many times. This tightens the weave and sets the width and length of the piece so that it won't shrink under ordinary use.

Another step is needed for fabrics that should have a soft fuzzy surface, like tweeds. The cloth passes between rollers with special burrs on them, the burrs pull up the yarn into a nap, which is then sheared off evenly by very sharp knives as the cloth goes between other rollers.

Finally the ends of the strips are sewed together into even longer strips and put through dry-cleaning machines. Oil, which was put into the wool to make it easier to work, is taken out and dirt or spots are removed. Then these strips, hundreds of feet long, are carried along overhead travelers, looking like moving belts, into vats of hot soapy water where they are washed again. After washing, the material is dried and pressed by passing over it big, slow-moving gas-heated cylinders. Finally it emerges, clean and wrinkle-free, and falls in loose folds into big baskets.

From here the material goes to the weave-room perch, where an inspector pulls the cloth slowly over a frame in front of him and inspects it carefully for any flaws or imperfections in weaving. If he finds one, he marks it in chalk, and the bolt goes to a repair frame, where skilled women reweave the imperfect places if possible. If not, the mill allows the purchaser a credit of one-eighth yard for each flaw.

Now at last the cloth is weighed, measured, folded into bolts, and wrapped for shipment to the customer.

COTTON

Eighty percent of the world's fabrics are woven from cotton, which got its name from the Arabic word *kotn*. It comes from a small bushlike plant with broad, three-cleft leaves. Cottonseeds grow in capsules, called bolls, which are surrounded by a soft, fuzzy, white fiber. This fiber is the part of the plant that is spun into cloth.

The American cotton belt, stretching from Georgia to California, is about 3000 miles long from east to west and 700 miles wide from north to south. It is the greatest producer of cotton in the world.

In colonial America cotton was grown in the

Southern colonies and shipped to the English mills. The British government tried in every way to discourage Americans from establishing mills of their own. They forbade English-trained weavers to emigrate to America, and made it illegal to export any spinning or weaving machinery, so it was many years before anybody on this side of the Atlantic could make cotton into cloth.

At the end of the eighteenth century an English weaver, named Samuel Slater, smuggled himself out of England and came to New England. There he built the first successful American cotton mill, at Pawtucket, Rhode Island, in 1790. He had to construct a spinning frame like Arkwright's and power looms like Cartwright's entirely from memory, but he succeeded in building and running the first water-powered spinning and weaving factory in the New World.

One of the great drawbacks of the American type of cotton was that the fiber clung stub-

bornly to the seeds, and it was hard to separate them. The seeds had to be removed by hand, usually by Negro slaves, who could clean only about a pound of cotton a day. The process was so slow that the price of cleaned cotton was a dollar a pound.

Then a Yankee graduate of Yale, named Eli Whitney, went South to tutor the son of a South Carolina planter. At Mulberry Grove, the plantation where he was to live, he first saw Negro slave women scratching the seeds from the raw cotton with their fingernails. Although he had never before seen a cotton boll or its seed, he decided to build a machine that would speed up this operation. Once again a man untrained in the textile industry invented a machine no one else had thought of.

Whitney covered the outside of a wooden cylinder with the teeth of a wire comb. He put the toothed roller below the cotton, which projected from an upper hopper made of iron mesh. The sawlike teeth on the roller clawed away the loose fibers from the coton bolls, holding the fibers and dropping the seeds through the grating of a hopper underneath. Then the brushes of a second roller, moving in the opposite direction, removed the cotton from the first cylinder.

Whitney's cotton gin, short for engine, immediately made an enormous difference in the size of the South's cotton crop. In 1793, because of the cost and slowness of picking the seeds by hand, only 487,000 pounds of cotton were exported. By 1811, when the gin was in general use, over 62,000,000 pounds were exported.

Eli Whitney had the same troubles as the earlier inventors in the cloth industry. A crowd of planters broke into the house where he kept his machine, copied it, and built their own gins without paying him anything. Not until seven years later did Whitney get a grant of $50,000, as a reward for inventing the machine that had made the fortunes of the Southern planters.

Today there are six kinds of cotton. The most valuable, a long-fibered cotton discovered by Columbus when he landed in the Bahamas, is called Sea Island. It was first raised commercially on the sea islands off the coast of South Carolina and Georgia, from seeds brought from the Bahamas. Very little is now raised. What there is of it is expensive and is used to make the finest high-quality cotton goods.

In order of their excellence the others are:

Egyptian Karnack—a long-fibered cotton grown along the Nile.

American Supima—developed in 1953 by combining American Pima, an American-Egyptian hybrid, with Sea Island cotton.

American Upland—a short-fibered cotton that makes up more than half of the world's crop. It grows in nearly all cotton regions.

Brazilian—a cotton much like American Upland.

Peruvian—a rough-fibered cotton that looks like wool and is often used in wool-and-cotton mixtures.

With a few differences, spinning cotton yarn and weaving the yarn into cloth is much like spinning wool yarn and making woolen fabrics.

All of the cotton plant is useful to mankind. Cotton fibers appear everywhere in the home. They are woven into rugs and carpets, into drapes and curtains, into slipcovers for furniture, and into towels and bedding. Half of the entire annual cotton crop is made into clothing for men, women, and children.

The automobile industry uses 160,000 bales for tires and upholstery. Cotton is needed to make electrical appliances, shoes, furniture, rubber goods, luggage, and tents. It is used by dairies, fisheries, and packing houses. The Army, Navy, and Air Force use cotton for uniforms, bedding, tents, hammocks, gun covers, and even for gunpowder.

The oil squeezed from the cottonseed is the second largest source of cooking oil, fat, and salad dressings in the United States. It also goes into the making of soap, paint, and lubricants. Even after the oil has been removed, the seed is useful as a meal or cake for feeding livestock and for fertilizer. The kernel of the seed is also ground into a flour rich in protein and vitamin B, and it is used to make breads, cakes, and candies. Even the hulls from which the seeds have been removed make good roughage to feed livestock, and they are useful in refining lubricating oils and in making plastics.

Finally, the linters, or fiber ends, which stick to the seeds and are mostly cellulose, can be spun into twine, carpets, and lampwicks. Also the chemical industry turns them into rayon, plastics, and lacquers.

Now if you should focus a microscope or reading glass upon a coat, dress, necktie, or stocking, you will have a better understanding of what went into the creation of the fabric. There is a cloth for every purpose, and each one adds to the diversity and comfort of our world today.

INDEX